1st Recital Series

PIANO ACCOMPANIMENT

FOR F HORN

Including works of:
- James Curnow
- Craig Alan
- Douglas Court
- Mike Hannickel
- Timothy Johnson
- Ann Lindsay

Solos for Beginning
through Early Intermediate
level musicians

CURNOW® MUSIC

EXCLUSIVELY DISTRIBUTED BY

HAL•LEONARD® CORPORATION

7777 W. BLUEMOUND RD. P.O. BOX 13819 MILWAUKEE, WI 53213

Edition Number: CMP 0762.02

1st Recital Series
Solos for Beginning through Early Intermediate level musicians
Piano Accompaniment for F Horn

ISBN: 90-431-1749-8

Foreword

High quality solo/recital literature that is appropriate for performers playing at the Beginner through Early Intermediate skill levels is finally here! Each of the **1st RECITAL SERIES** books is loaded with exciting and varied solo pieces that have been masterfully composed or arranged for your instrument.

Included with the solo book there is a professionally recorded CD that demonstrates each piece. Use these examples to help develop proper performance practices. There is also a recording of the accompaniment alone that can be used for performance (and rehearsal) when a live accompanist is not available. A separate solo F Horn book is available [edition nr. CMP 0761.02].

Table of Contents

1. SHADOWS OF THE PAST

Mike Hannickel (ASCAP)

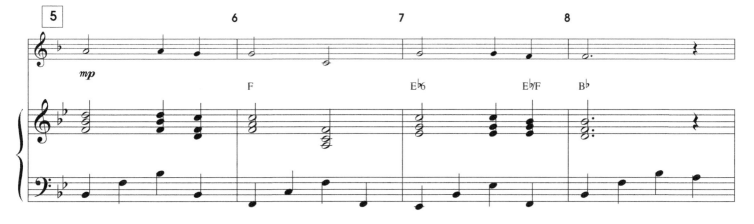

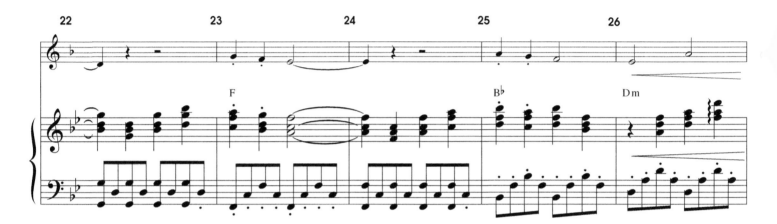

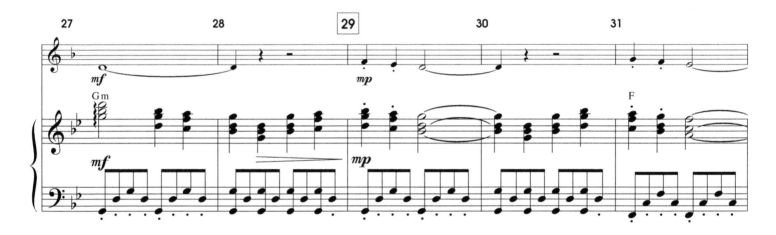

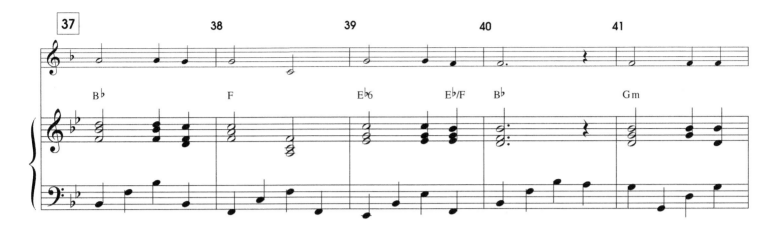

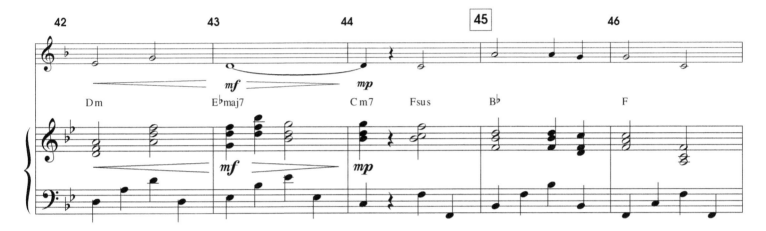

F HORN

2. ANCIENT TOWERS

Craig Alan (ASCAP)

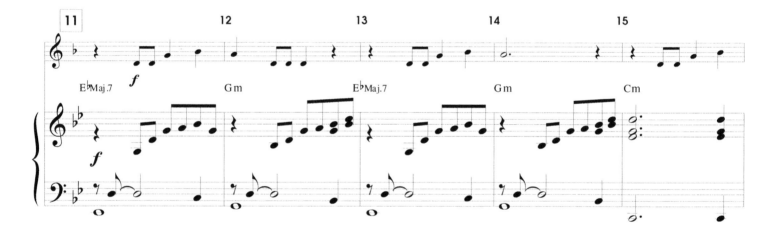

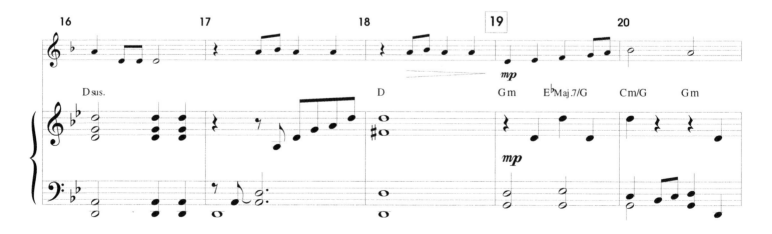

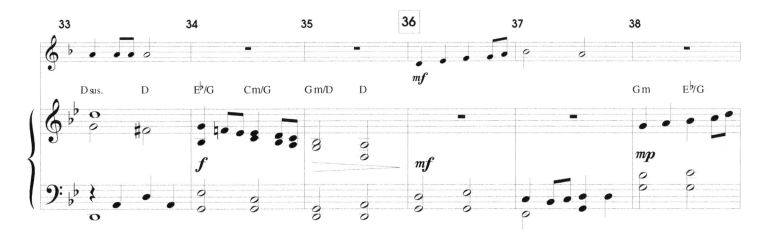

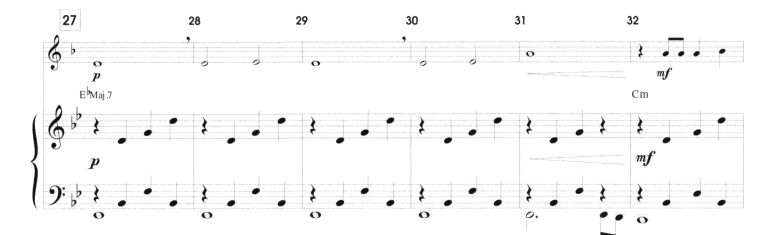

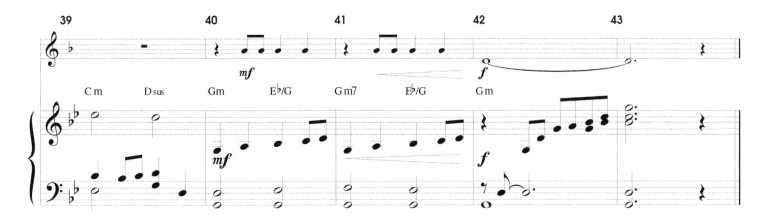

3. ANTHEM

Mike Hannickel (ASCAP)

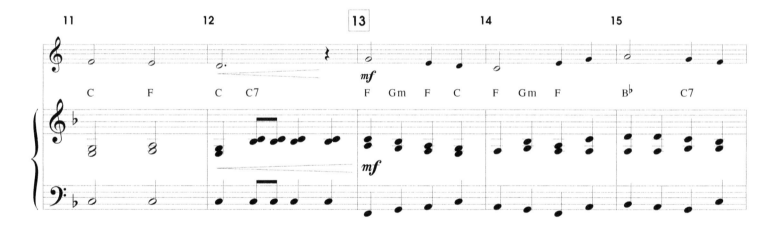

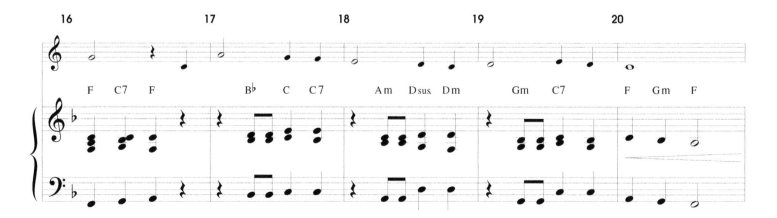

Copyright © 2002 by **Curnow Music Press, Inc.**

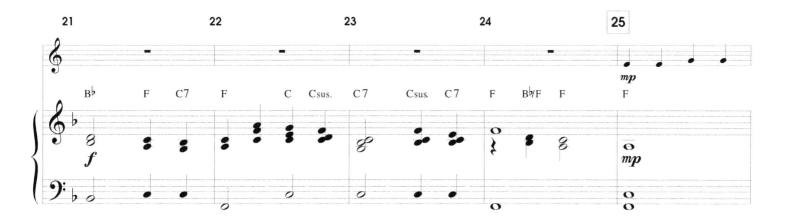

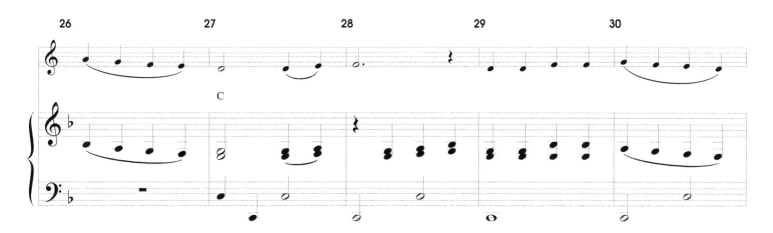

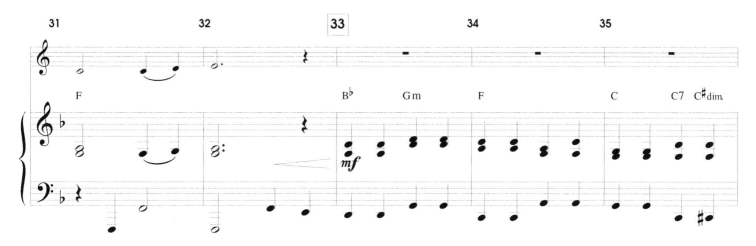

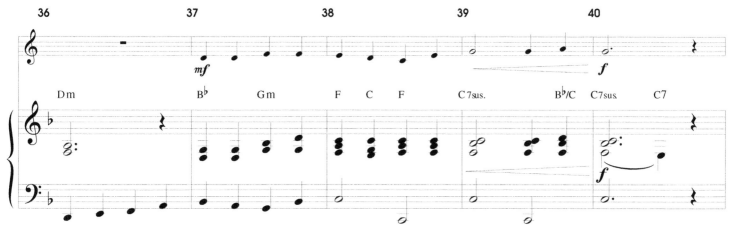

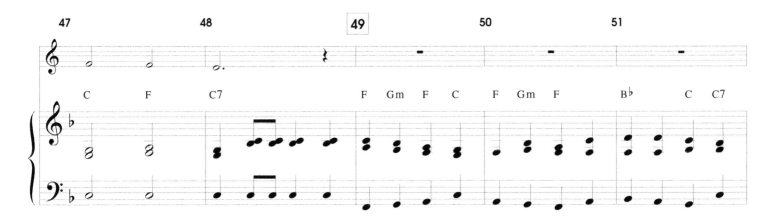

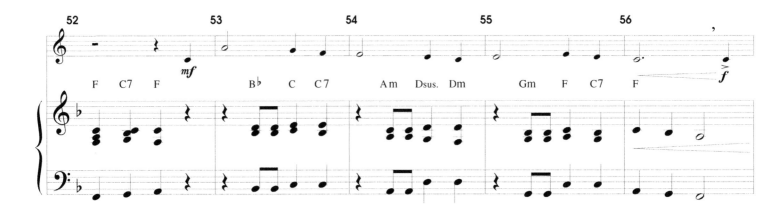

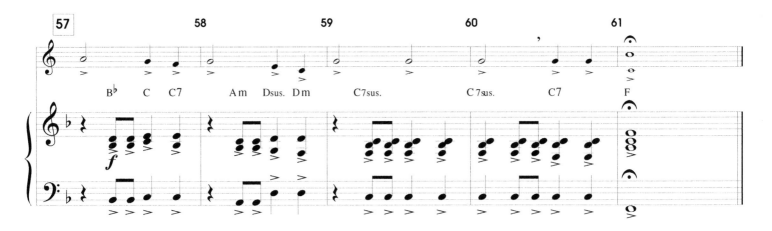

4. EVENING SHADOWS

Timothy Johnson (ASCAP)

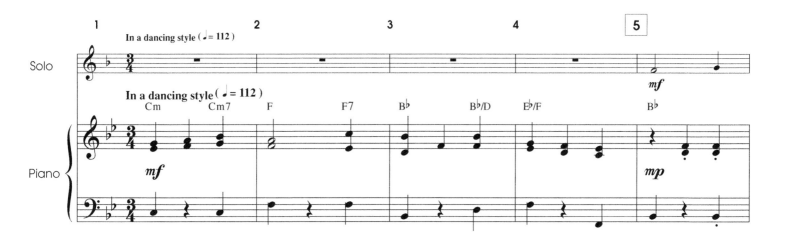

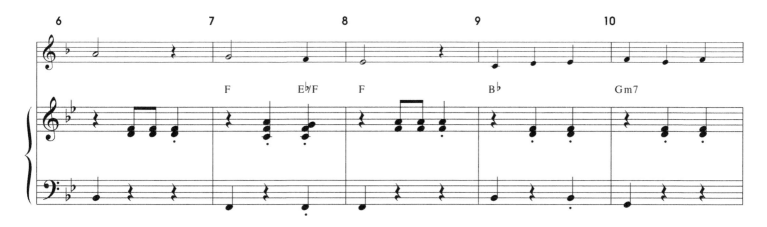

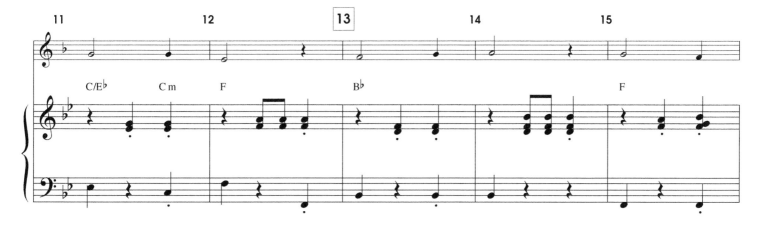

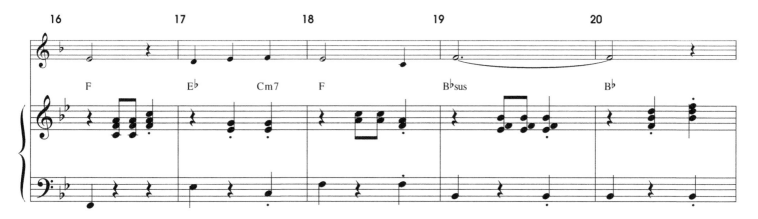

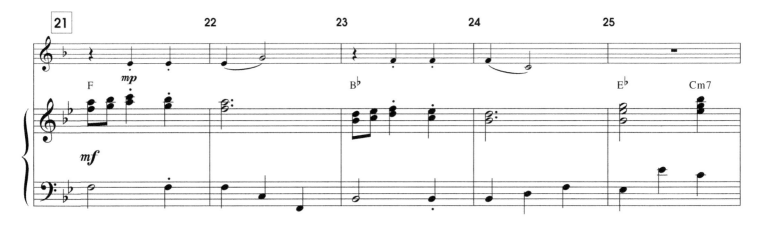

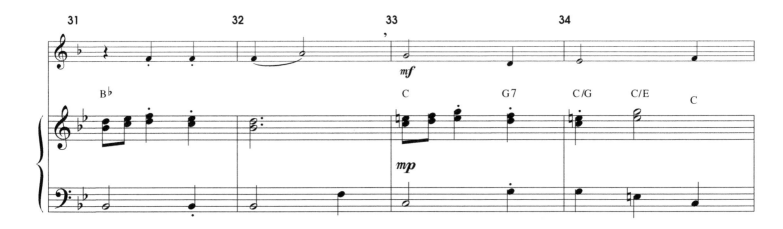

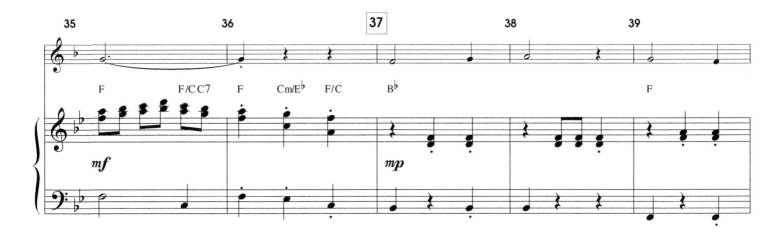

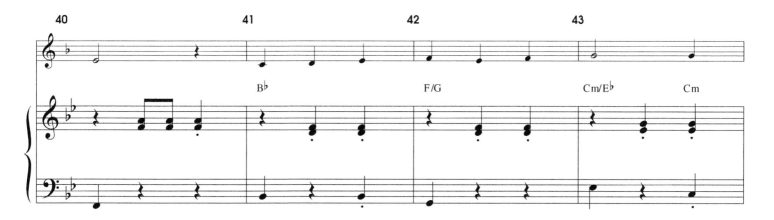

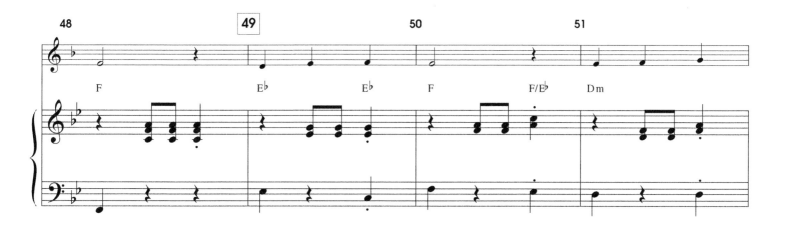

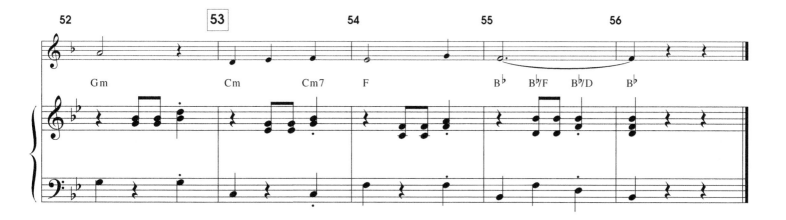

Franz Schubert
5. SANCTUS

F HORN

Arr. **James Curnow** (ASCAP)

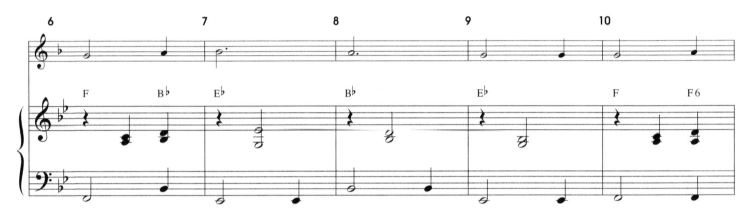

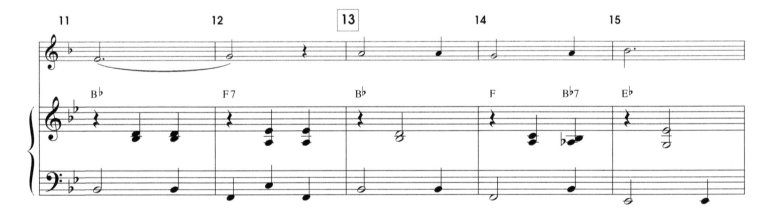

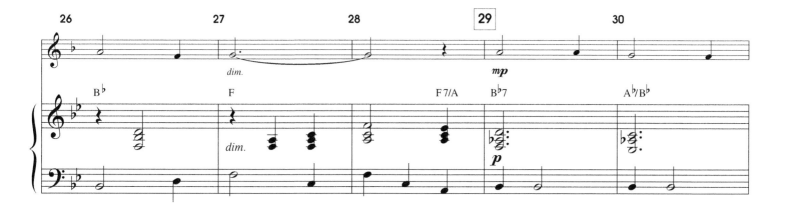

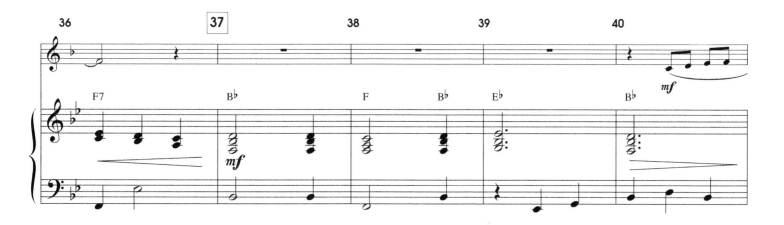

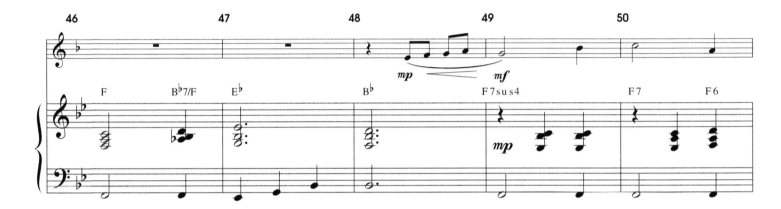

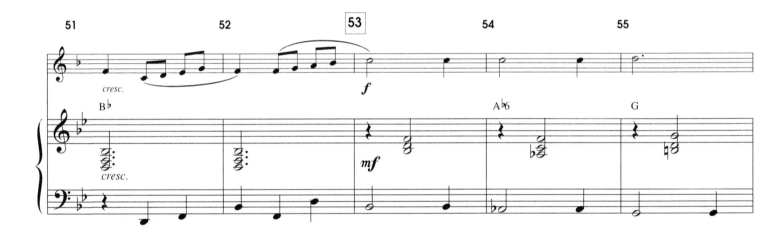

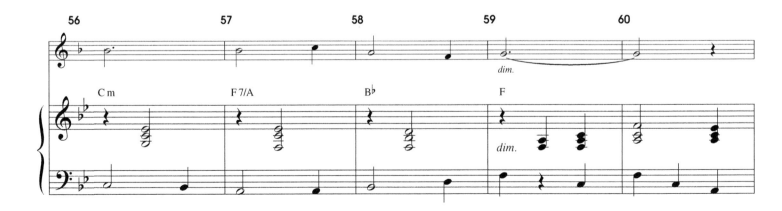

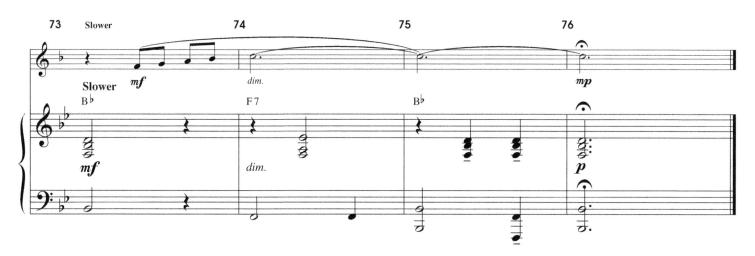

6. TRUMPET VOLUNTARY

Jeremiah Clarke
Arr. **Ann Lindsay** (ASCAP)

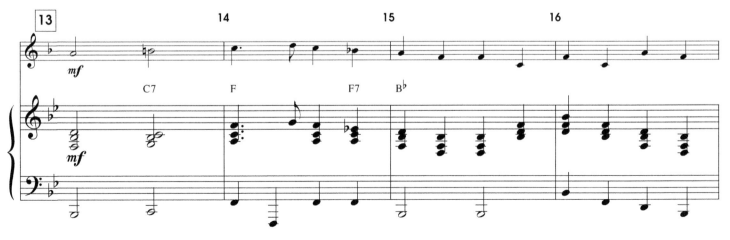

7. COPPER AND ZINC

Ann Lindsay (ASCAP)

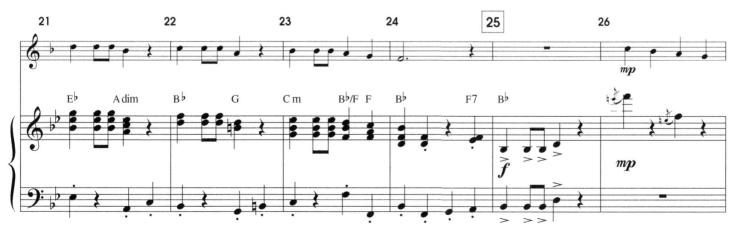

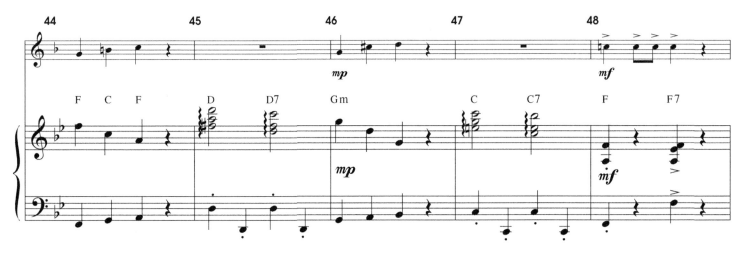

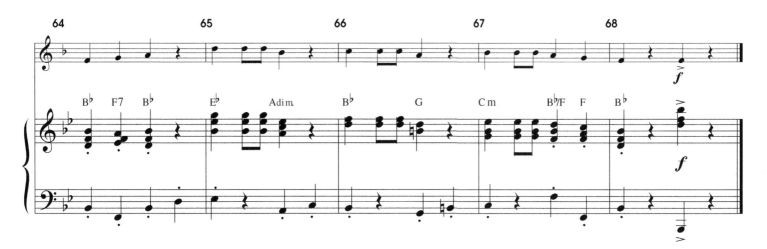

8. MARCH MAJESTIC

Douglas Court (ASCAP)

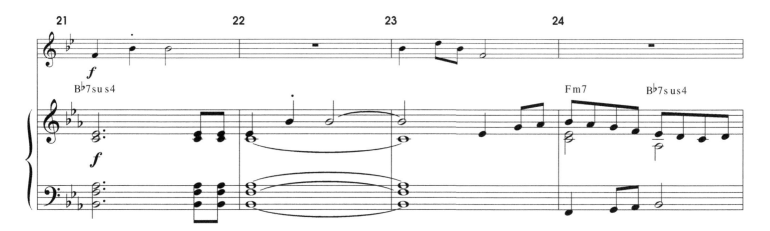

9. THE BRITISH GRENADIERS

Traditional
Arr. **James Curnow** (ASCAP)

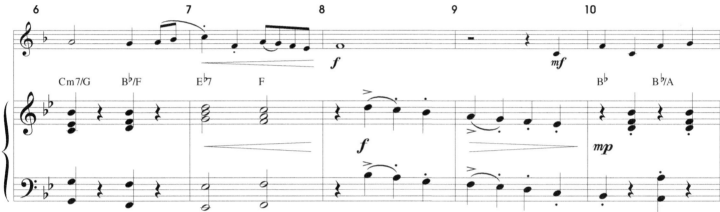

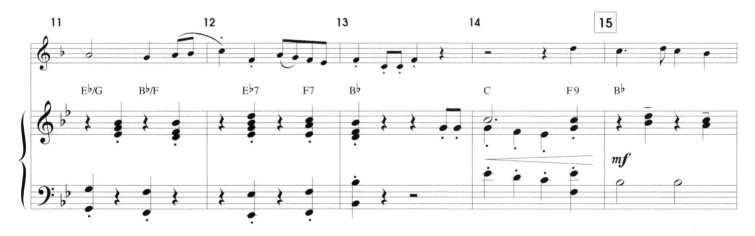

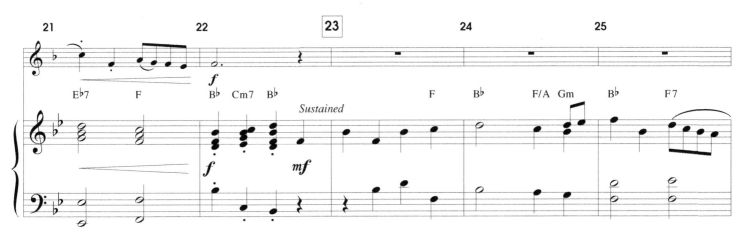

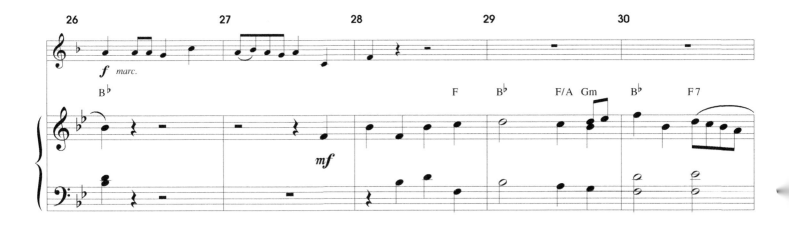

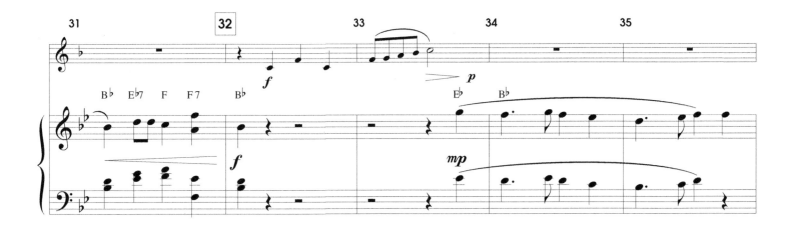

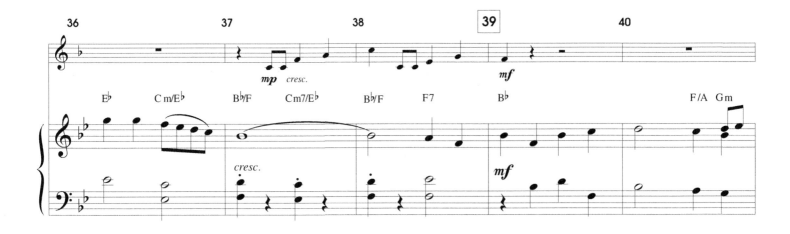

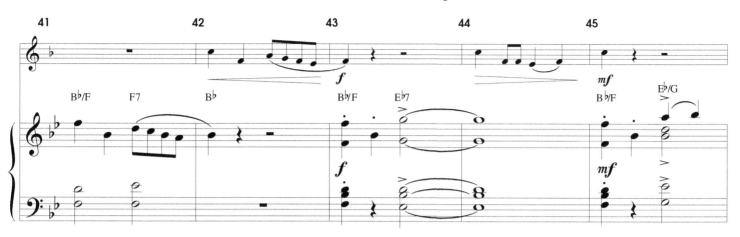

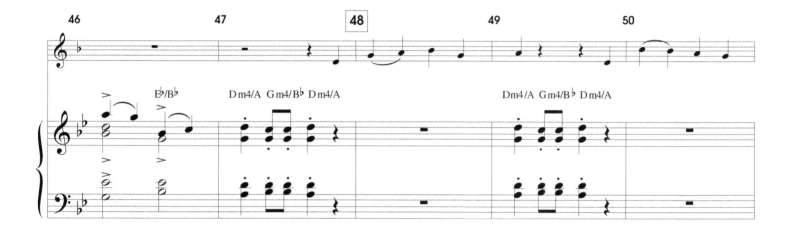

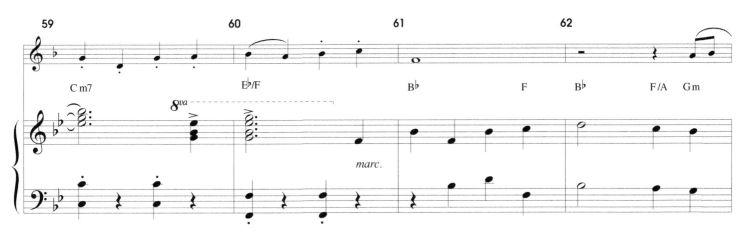

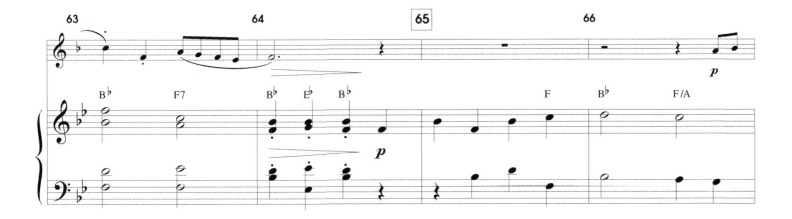

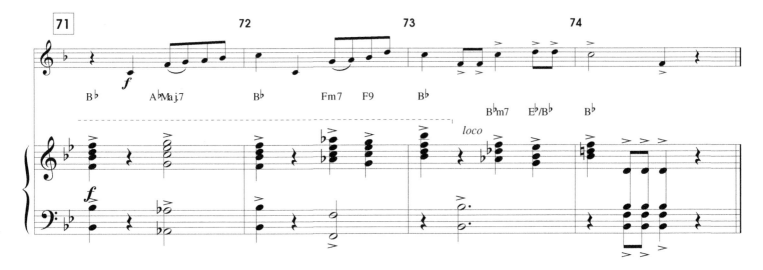

10. THE RED BALLOON

James Curnow (ASCAP)

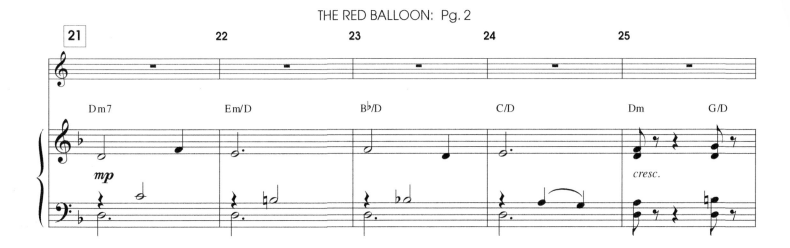

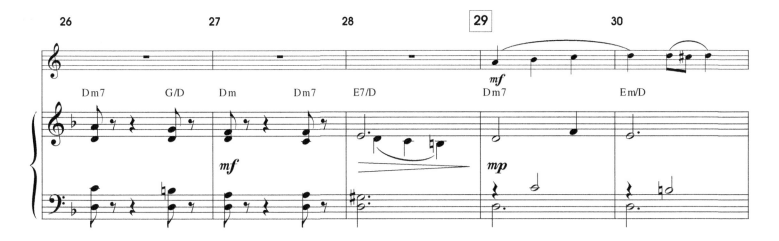

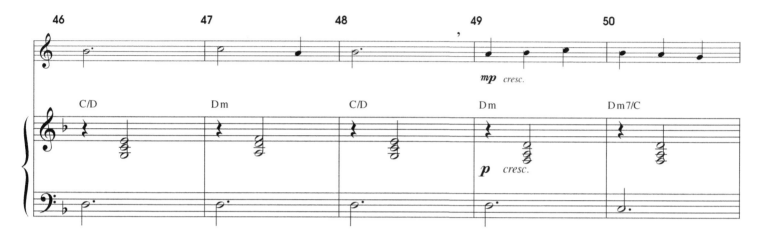

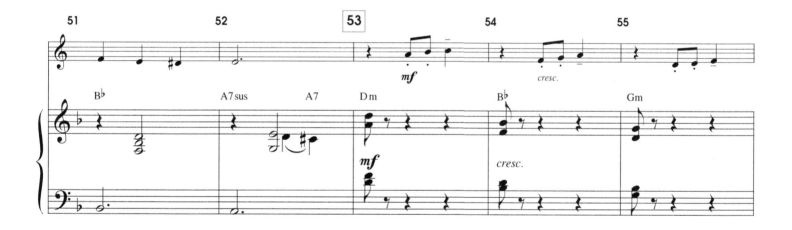

11. EXCURSION

Timothy Johnson (ASCAP)

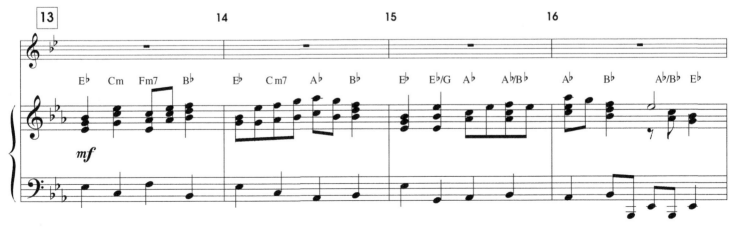

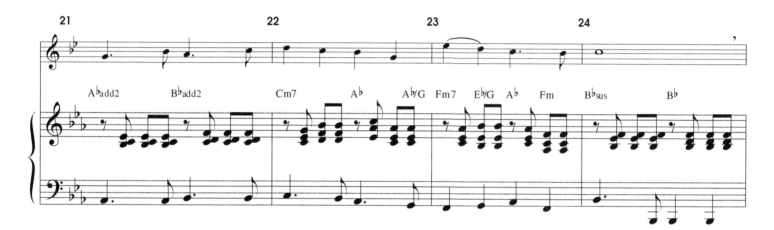

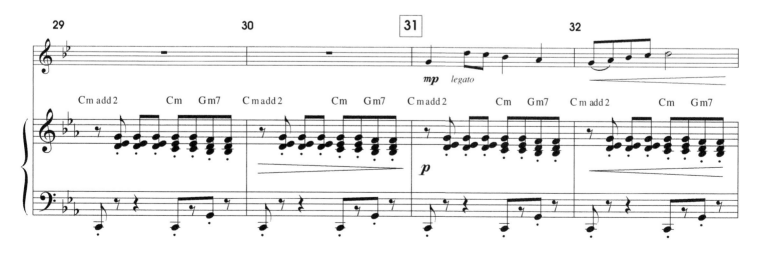

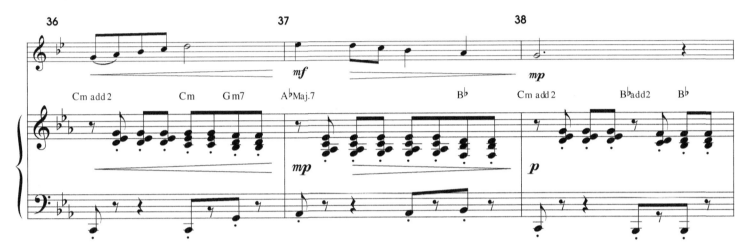

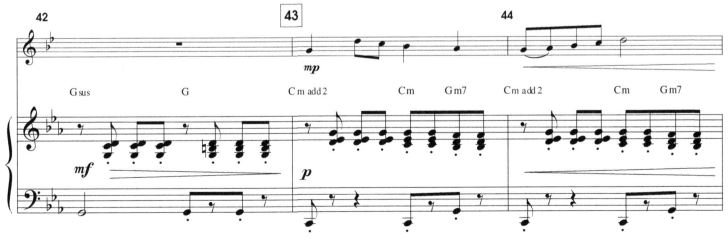

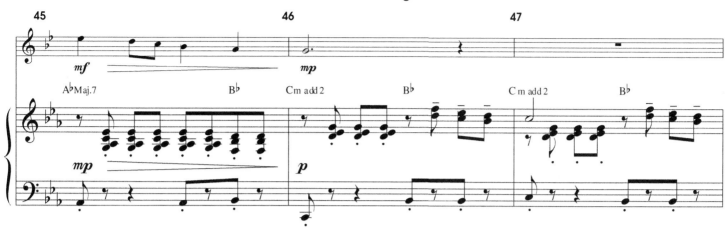

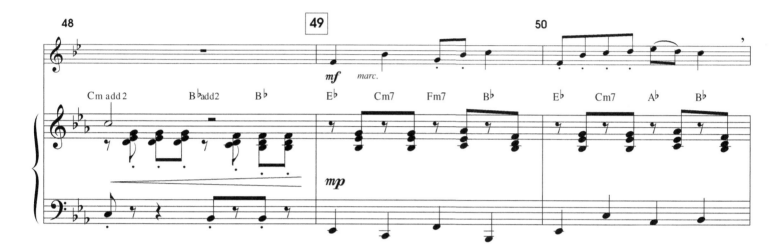

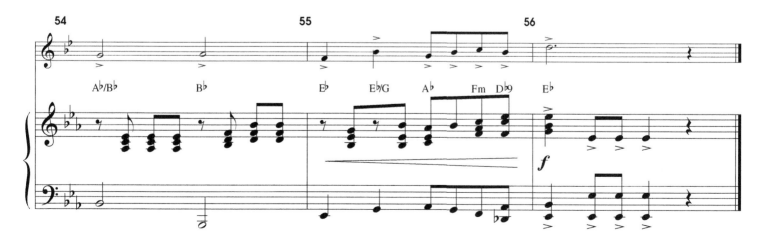

W. A. Mozart
12. ANDANTE
from LA CI DAREM LA MANO
From Don Giovanni

Arr. **Ann Lindsay** (ASCAP)

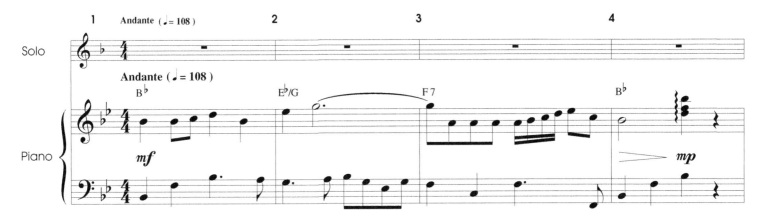

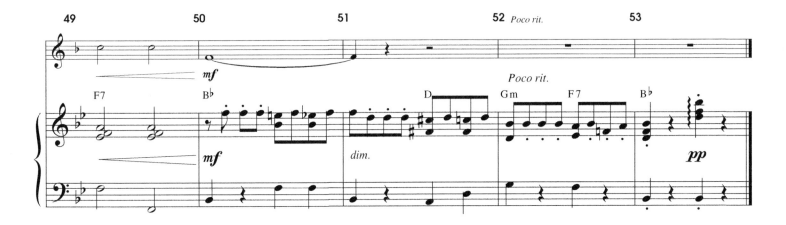